Baby animal names
Nombres de animales bebé

Bobbie Kalman

 Crabtree Publishing Company
www.crabtreebooks.com

Created by Bobbie Kalman

Author and Editor-in-Chief
Bobbie Kalman

Educational consultants
Reagan Miller
Elaine Hurst
Joan King

Editors
Joan King
Reagan Miller
Kathy Middleton

Proofreader
Crystal Sikkens

Design
Bobbie Kalman
Katherine Berti

Photo research
Bobbie Kalman

Production coordinator
Katherine Berti

Prepress technician
Katherine Berti

Photographs
BigStockPhoto: p. 10
Other photographs by Shutterstock

Library and Archives Canada Cataloguing in Publication

Available at Library and Archives Canada

Library of Congress Cataloging-in-Publication Data

Available at Library of Congress

Crabtree Publishing Company
www.crabtreebooks.com   1-800-387-7650

Printed in China/082010/AP20100512

Published in Canada
Crabtree Publishing
616 Welland Ave.
St. Catharines, Ontario
L2M 5V6

Published in the United States
Crabtree Publishing
PMB 59051
350 Fifth Avenue, 59th Floor
New York, New York 10118

Published in the United Kingdom
Crabtree Publishing
Maritime House
Basin Road North, Hove
BN41 1WR

Published in Australia
Crabtree Publishing
386 Mt. Alexander Rd.
Ascot Vale (Melbourne)
VIC 3032

Words to know
Palabras que debo saber

bear cub
osezno

fox kit or pup
cachorro de
zorro o cría

goat kid
cabrito

koala joey
cría de koala

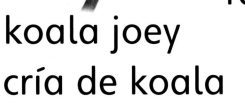

raccoon kittens
crías de
mapaches

wolf cub
lobato

Children are called **kids**.

A los niños se les llama **chicos**.

Baby **goats** are called kids, too.

Las **cabras** bebé se llaman cabritos.

Baby **cats** are called **kittens**.

Los **gatos** bebé se llaman **gatitos**.

Did you know that baby **raccoons** are called kittens, too?

¿Sabías que los **mapaches** bebé se llaman también crías?

A baby **dog** is called a **puppy**.

Un **perro** bebé se llama **cachorro**.

Did you know that a baby **fox**
is called a **pup** or a **kit**?

¿Sabías que un **zorro** bebé
se llama **cachorro** o **cría**?

Did you know that a baby **wolf** is called a pup or a **cub**?

¿Sabías que un **lobo** bebé se llama cachorro o **lobato**?

Did you know that a baby **bear** is also called a cub?

¿Sabías que un **oso** bebé se llama también osezno?

A baby **kangaroo** is called a **joey**.
The joey lives in its mother's **pouch**.

Un **canguro** bebé se llama **cría**.
La cría vive en el **marsupio** de su madre.

pouch
marsupio

Did you know
that a baby **koala**
is called a joey, too?
The baby koala also
lives in its mother's pouch.

¿Sabías que un **koala** bebé
se llama cría también?
El koala bebé también vive
en el marsupio de su madre.

13

Activity

How many baby
animal names
do you know?

Actividad

¿Cuántos nombres
de animales
bebé conoces?

A baby rabbit
is called a **bunny**.

Un conejo bebé
se llama **gazapo**.

A baby horse
is called a **foal**.

Un caballo bebé
se llama **potrillo**.

A baby sheep
is called a **lamb**.

Una oveja bebé
se llama **cordero**.

A baby deer
is called a **fawn**.

Un ciervo bebé
se llama **cervato**.

A baby giraffe
is called a **calf**.

Una jirafa bebé
se llama **becerro**.

Notes for adults

What's in a name?
Baby animal names helps children learn the names of animals and what they are called as babies. Ask the children if they think baby goats are like children and if raccoons are like cats, since they share the same baby names. Make a list of all the nicknames the children were called when they were babies.

Animal match-ups
Create an animal match-up game to help reinforce new animal vocabulary and place memory. Create a set of cards with pictures showing the baby animals in the book. On a separate set of cards, write the name of the baby animal (kit, joey, cub, foal, calf). Lay out the cards face down on the floor. Ask the students to take turns turning over two cards to make as many matches as they can.

Notas para los adultos

¿Qué dice un nombre?
Nombres de animales bebé ayuda a los niños a aprender los nombres de los animales y como se llaman cuando son bebés. Pregúnteles a los niños si piensan que los perros bebé son como los zorros bebé y si los canguros se parecen a los koalas, ya que comparten los mismos nombres de bebé. Haga una lista de los apodos que los niños tenían cuando eran bebés.

Emparejar animales
Cree un juego de emparejar animales para reforzar el vocabulario nuevo sobre los animales y la memoria. Haga un juego de tarjetas con figuras que muestren los animales bebé del libro. En un juego adicional de tarjetas escriba el nombre de los animales bebé (cría, cachorro, lobato, potrillo, cabrito). Coloque las tarjetas boca abajo en el suelo. Pida a los estudiantes que se turnen y volteen dos tarjetas para formar cuantas parejas puedan.